DOGS ON DUTY

BY CATHERINE O'NEILL

BOOKS FOR WORLD EXPLORERS
NATIONAL GEOGRAPHIC SOCIETY

CONTENTS

▷ TINY ENOUGH *to ride in a clown's oversize jeans, Chihuahuas Spotty and Bunny earn their living making people laugh.*

TITLE PAGE: *A Border collie takes a break during the Welsh National Sheepdog Trials. The trials test herding ability, and determine the top 15 sheepdogs in Wales, Scotland, and England.*

COVER: *At Krabloonik, a kennel in the Colorado mountains, Jessica Starodoj, 12, discovers that sled dogs make affectionate friends as well as good workers.*

DAVID HISER

Copyright © 1988 National Geographic Society
Library of Congress CIP Data: Page 104

OUR BEST FRIENDS

AN INTRODUCTION

When a dog owner returns home at the end of the day, there's something special waiting: a joyous bark, a wagging tail, and a greeting fit for a long-lost friend.

People and dogs have been together for a long, long time—about 12,000 years. The first dogs to be domesticated, or tamed, probably were wolflike animals that followed traveling bands of hunters. Staying close to humans gave the early dogs an easy food source—the scraps the hunters left behind.

The humans discovered that when strangers or wild animals approached, dogs barked a warning. They began to rely on the dogs to help guard their camps and their livestock. People and dogs began spending a lot of time together.

Over the centuries, dogs proved that, with training, they could perform many duties. They helped find food, herded sheep, and hauled crops to market. Today, dogs act as eyes or ears or legs for the disabled. They rescue people in danger and help police catch criminals. Dogs are good at many things. The most important, perhaps, is just being our friends.

▽ YOUR BOOT? *This dog is doing what comes naturally: fetching. The golden retriever was first bred in the British Isles as a hunting dog. Now people all over the world find it an intelligent, gentle pet.*

◁ BEST FRIENDS. *A Samoyed puppy shares a quiet moment with Peter Wilkinson, 8, of Saint-Lambert, Quebec, in Canada. Affectionate and loyal, dogs are popular pets. About 56 million live in homes across North America.*

△ HURRY HOME. *A snowy day doesn't stop Sylva, a mixed breed, from peering eagerly over a gate for her owner's return. Dogs depend on humans for companionship and love. When the owner arrives, Sylva will jump with joy.*

DOGS
SHARING THE WORK

Sheep graze peacefully as a large dog rests nearby. Although there is no shepherd in sight, the sheep are safe. The presence of the watchful dog keeps attackers away.

Long ago, on the high, windswept plains of Asia, dogs similar to the Italian maremma on these pages were already guarding livestock for their human owners. Like the maremma, the dogs were ideally suited to their jobs. Their thick, shaggy coats enabled them to survive bitterly cold winters. Their pale color did not frighten the sheep or cause shepherds to mistake them for predators. Their strength and size enabled them to defend their flock against any attacker.

Later, dogs of this kind spread to Europe, where today their descendants work in many countries—the komondor and the kuvasz in Hungary, the Great Pyrenees in France, and other breeds elsewhere. All big and strong, they have one aim: to guard their flocks.

Like their ancestors, livestock-guarding dogs of today live with their herds. From the time they are puppies, the dogs form a strong

WITH TOM ON GUARD, *sheep nibble grass in a field at the Hampshire College Farm Center, in Amherst, Massachusetts. Tom is a maremma, a type of guard dog bred long ago in Italy to protect sheep from predators—especially wolves.*

attachment to the livestock. Just as a pet dog often looks out for its owner, a loyal guard dog looks out for its sheep, goats, or cattle.

Over the years, livestock-guarding breeds have developed special ways of behaving. Most important, they do not attack the sheep. They stay with the animals they guard. And they will protect their livestock no matter what happens.

Sheep farmers Lu and Jan Wilts found out just how far a guard dog will go to protect its sheep when a pack of coyotes attacked their flock. The sheep were grazing high in the Colorado mountains. They were watched over by a big komondor named Hagar. Although no one saw the attack, it was obvious from Hagar's condition afterward that he had held off several coyotes trying to kill some of the sheep.

When the fight was all over, Hagar was a mess—but not one sheep or lamb was missing. Luckily, the dog's thick fur had protected him. He was exhausted and covered with shallow bites, but he was very much alive. After his injuries healed, Hagar was right back out guarding his flock. Says Jan Wilts, "It's impressive to observe the mutual trust and affection that exist between Hagar and the sheep."

Until the 1980s, few livestock-guarding dogs could be found in the United States. Although farmers and ranchers worked hard to prevent wild animal attacks on their flocks, livestock losses were heavy. In 1979, for example, predators destroyed nearly 1.3 million sheep.

Then, European livestock-guarding dogs were introduced. In just a few years, they became valuable workers. And they didn't hurt the environment or destroy harmless wild animals—unlike the poisons, traps, and guns often used to control predators.

To study how effective guard dogs can be, researchers at the Livestock (Continued on page 12)

◁ **ON THE ROAD** *in New Zealand, a man on horseback teams up with three dogs to keep a herd of cattle moving. If a car approaches, the dogs will quickly move the cattle to the side of the road.*

▽ **HITCHING A RIDE** *after a long day, a New Zealand herding dog gets a break from its routine. Riding with the stockman saves the dog from crossing the rocky riverbed, where it might injure its paws.*

LUIS CASTAÑEDA/IMAGE BANK

JOHN EASTCOTT AND YVA MOMATIUK/WOODFIN CAMP & ASSOCIATES (LEFT)   BRUCE FOSTER/WILDLIGHT

△ **CROSSING A RIVER** *with a flock of sheep in Spain is all in a day's work for this dog. All over the world, dogs of many breeds—and mixed-breed dogs like this one—help shepherds keep their flocks moving safely.*

◁ A WATCHFUL PAIR *of Border collies keeps a flock in order on a farm in Wales. Next, Stephen Davies-Russell and the dogs will run the sheep through a disinfectant footbath.*

△ GOOD DOG. *Philip Davies-Russell, a full-time dog trainer in Wales, praises Ben for a job well done. Philip has worked with sheepdogs all his life.*

△ FUZZY BUDDIES. *A playful kitten teases a Border collie pup on a farm in England.*

(Continued from page 9) Dog Project, at Hampshire College, in Massachusetts, have placed hundreds of dogs on farms and ranches in 39 states. So far, the results are encouraging. Where guard dogs go, safety seems to follow. Studies have shown that when a dog works under conditions it has been bred for, losses to coyotes and other attackers fall an average of 77 percent. Most predators will not risk coming up to a flock while a dog is on duty. Only rarely do guard dogs have to fight. When they do, they're well equipped to win—as Hagar's owners found.

While some breeds are best suited for protecting livestock from harm, other breeds have become masters at driving animals from pasture to pasture. These are the herding dogs. Intelligent and quick, they can move hundreds of animals over hundreds of miles—without losing a single one.

In Australia, several types of herding dogs have been developed. One is the agile kelpie, which helps people on horseback move enormous flocks long distances in the outback—the vast, nearly deserted heart of the Australian continent. Many other breeds make good herding dogs. Border collies, originally bred in the highlands of the British Isles, are among the best.

Shepherds and their dogs have been partners in the sheep business since the days of the Egyptian pharaohs. So it's not surprising that certain dogs are born with the instinct to herd animals; they've been doing it for thousands of years. A Border collie puppy will try to herd just about anything that moves—lambs, chicks, insects, even the ripples on a pond. Serious training to develop that instinct into the skill required of a professional herder begins when the dog is about six months old. At that time, a young dog may (Continued on page 16)

JOANNA B. PINNEO (ALL)

▽ **FAMILY PORTRAIT.** *Collies crowd around Garrick in a field. These and three other Border collies work with about 170 sheep on the Terrys' farm. Garrick trained Jean, his own dog, which is at his right hand.*

▷ **HELLO, LAMB.** *Garrick introduces a month-old lamb to Tip, one of the family dogs. Collies have an instinct to herd sheep. If Garrick put this lamb down, Tip would make sure it didn't wander away.*

△ CROUCHING LOW, *Mindy keeps sheep in line as Garrick Terry works. "Mindy keeps the sheep away while I spread feed," he says. "Otherwise, they crowd around and bump me." Garrick's family runs a sheep farm in Hillsboro, Virginia.*

MIKE ABRAHAMS (BOTH)

△ DRIVING SHEEP *across a field is part of the routine at the Welsh National Sheepdog Trials. This dog was one of 144 to take part in the trials, which lasted three days. The best 15 dogs go on to compete in the International Trial.*

▽ PENNING *tests the skills of a dog and its handler at the Welsh trials. The sheep don't look too interested in moving— but they will. On a farm, the dogs often have to drive flocks into pens for shearing or for medical attention.*

TEAMWORK ON TRIAL

At a national trial event, it's skill, speed, and teamwork between dog and handler that count. Here's what happens:

1 *At a signal, the dog leaves its handler. It loops around and stops behind five sheep, two of which wear ribbons.*

2 *Careful not to upset the sheep, the dog starts them moving toward the handler.*

3 *Still working behind the sheep, the dog moves them through an obstacle and on toward the handler.*

4 *Driving the sheep around the handler, the dog heads them into a turn, through two more obstacles, called drive panels, and back to the handler.*

5 *The handler then maneuvers two of the unribboned sheep together. The dog separates those two from the others and moves them to the shedding ring.*

6 *Finally, the dog rounds up all the sheep and drives them into a pen. The handler shuts the pen gate behind them.*

② LIFT

400 YARDS

ROZ SCHANZER (ART)

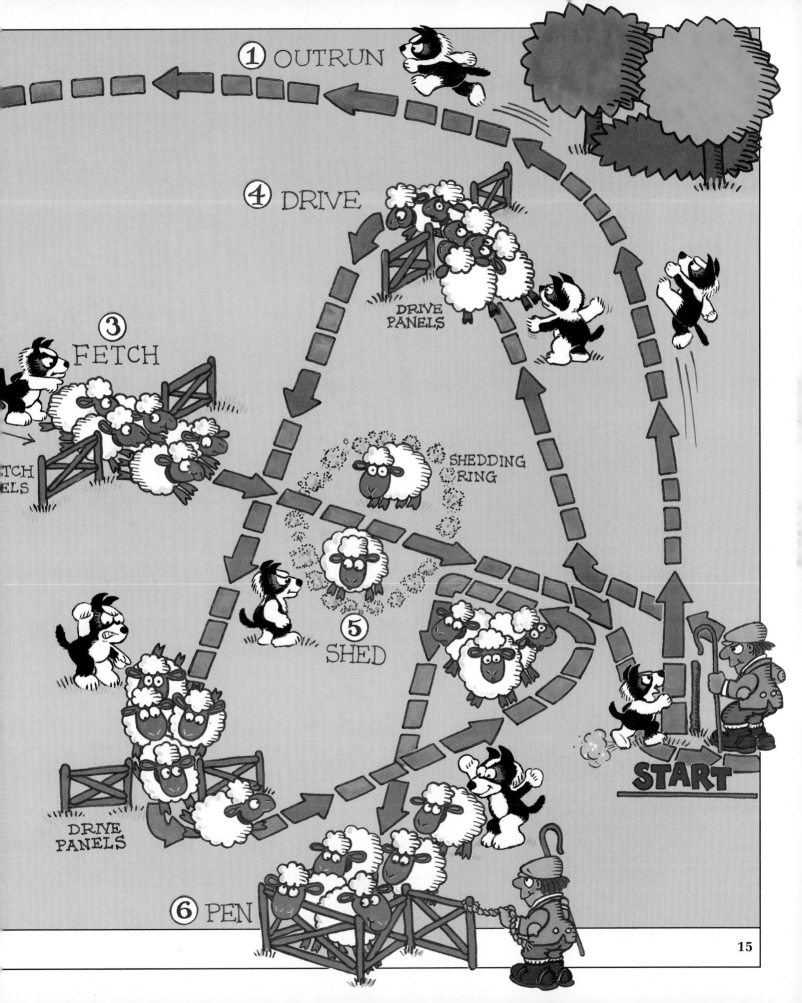

① OUTRUN

④ DRIVE

DRIVE PANELS

③ FETCH

TCH ELS

SHEDDING RING

⑤ SHED

DRIVE PANELS

⑥ PEN

START

15

(Continued from page 12) simply be put out in a field to learn from older, more experienced dogs. In other cases, a human trainer may work with the dog.

At first, training sessions last 10 or 15 minutes. The shepherd works the dog with a few sheep. The dog quickly learns to respond to voice signals, hand signals, or a combination of the two. A shepherd also may use a whistle to signal a dog. After about six months of training, most sheepherding dogs are ready to begin working the flocks.

In the field, the dog learns to drive—move the sheep from place to place. It learns to gather the sheep—round them up and bring them to the shepherd. Finally, it learns to herd sheep into a pen and to separate individual animals from the flock.

Herd dogs work sheep by crouching down and moving toward them. To sheep, the stalking herd dog looks like an attacking predator. The dog's

▷ **"WOOLWALKING"** *comes naturally to an Australian kelpie. The dog will walk over the sheep's backs, then dive into the mob to clear traffic jams.*

▽ *A JILLEROO, or female Australian sheep station hand, uses a motorbike to transport lambs—and a sheepdog.*

color, usually dark, triggers the instinct to move away. The sheep get going. The dog controls their direction with its movements, guiding the sheep from place to place. It nips at their heels and sometimes jumps across their backs to recapture a stray.

Herd dogs also control sheep by a method called "using eye." The dog stares at the sheep with a steady, hypnotizing look. A herding dog uses its eyes this way even when it's a puppy. After the dog goes to work, sheep quickly learn to do what it wants when the dog looks at them.

Once a herd dog is trained, it works as part of a team with the shepherd. One person cannot control a herd of sheep; but a shepherd and a dog working together can do the work of a dozen people. Many shepherds and their dogs communicate so well that an onlooker can barely tell that the human is signaling to the dog. Yet the dog is completely under the shepherd's control. Spectators who attend sheepdog trials see this relationship in action.

The first sheepdog trial, or competition, was held in Wales, in 1873. In 1906, the International Sheepdog Society was founded. This organization has been growing ever since. Today, trials are held in Australia, North America, South America, and Europe, as well as in the United Kingdom and Ireland.

At a sheepdog trial, compact Border collies and some other breeds compete at what they do best: herding sheep. The trials are not just for show. The dogs work hard for their prizes. Here's what happens at a typical sheepdog trial:

With a voice or whistle command, a handler sends a dog racing 400 yards across a large field toward a group of five sheep. At some trials, the dog can't even see the sheep from its starting position.

As the signal sounds, the dog streaks toward the sheep. It must gather them and drive them through a

PETER KORNISS

◁ **A HEAVY MAT** *of tangled fur that reaches to the ground weatherproofs this komondor as it guards a sheep shed in Hungary. Komondors stand more than two feet tall and weigh up to 120 pounds.*

▽ SHEEP OR DOG? *In its woolly coat, a komondor guard dog resembles a sheep. It easily blends in with the flock.*

▷ SHAGGY HERO. *At a ranch near Florissant, Colorado, Jake Jennings, 9, pets Hagar, a komondor. That's Hagar's son Zephyr at right. The dogs' long hair has been cut. All alone, Hagar once held off a pack of attacking coyotes and saved his flock of sheep. "We didn't lose a single tuft of wool that night," says Jan Wilts, Hagar's owner.*

ANIMALS ANIMALS/ROBERT PEARCY

DAVID HISER (RIGHT)

18

set of gates into a small pen. But that's not the end of the event. The dog has to shed, or separate, a certain number of sheep from the rest. This isn't easy. Sheep by nature stay together. The dog is judged by the speed and style of its moves as it drives the sheep through the course. It also is judged by the number of signals it needs from its handler.

Once a champion dog gets through the local, national, and international qualifying levels of the trials, it faces an even greater challenge. In the Supreme Championship, the dog must run 750 yards and maneuver 20 sheep through the complicated gates and pens of the course. The winner of this trial takes the world's top sheepdog title. The supreme champion probably wouldn't win a prize in an ordinary dog show, though. Sheepdogs are bred for their intelligence and speed rather than for their looks. Brains, not beauty, count when it comes to working livestock.

◁ **THAT'S NO GOOSE!** *In a farmyard in Hungary, a kuvasz guards a flock of geese. The birds keep their distance from their furry protector.*

▽ **PULI PAIR.** *Quick and light, these Hungarian herders sometimes control runaway sheep by leaping on their backs and riding them until they tire.*

PETER KORNISS (BOTH)

DOGS
GIVING
A HAND

As traffic comes to a halt at a busy intersection, a Labrador retriever steps off the curb. The dog walks confidently to the other side of the street. His owner, a blind college student, walks just behind him, holding on to the handle of the dog's leather harness.

For the student, owning a well-trained dog guide means freedom and independence. The student can go to and from class without depending on anyone else for help.

Working in partnership with a dog guide, a blind person can go almost anywhere a sighted person can. Together, dog and owner walk up and down stairs. They board subways and buses. They go to restaurants. The dog acts as the blind person's eyes, guiding its owner safely wherever they go.

Dog guides for the blind are probably the most familiar of the service dogs. But did you know that dogs also act as ears for the deaf? Hearing dogs learn to notice such important sounds as those made by alarm clocks, doorbells, smoke detectors, sirens, and crying babies. They alert their owners to a noise,

SURE STEPS *of a golden Labrador retriever guide a blind person along a sidewalk. Since dog guides for the blind were introduced in the United States, during the 1920s, thousands of the animals have improved the lives of their blind owners.*

and let them know where the sound is coming from.

Dogs can be helpful partners for physically disabled people, too. At Canine Companions for Independence, in Santa Rosa, California, dogs learn to respond to 89 commands. These dogs can push elevator buttons with their paws and pull wheelchairs up steep walkways. They carry their owners' belongings in special dogpacks, open and close doors, turn on lights, and even pay for purchases. For some disabled children, having a canine companion gives them the chance to go places they've never gone before. The dogs often enable adults to take jobs and live on their own for the first time.

At some hospitals and nursing homes, dog visitors actually help improve the physical as well as the mental health of patients. Researchers have discovered that stroking an animal lowers a person's blood pressure. Because high blood pressure can lead to many illnesses, including heart disease, petting a dog can be good medicine. Some experts think that touching an animal may release chemicals in the human brain that make people relax and feel good.

Some nursing homes allow elderly residents to keep their own pets. In others, volunteers bring trained "therapy dogs" to visit on a regular basis. Some of these dogs have worked wonders. The elderly people look forward to the dogs' visits. One 90-year-old woman had stopped caring about life. She just stayed in bed. But once dogs became frequent visitors, she was always up and dressed, eager to greet them.

Older people who live on their own can also benefit from keeping a dog. Studies have shown that elderly pet owners stay healthier and happier than people who don't keep pets. Dog owners are more likely to eat regular (Continued on page 28)

◁ **BEST FRIENDS** *Andrew Cosel, 14, of Setauket, New York, and Charger go everywhere together. A group called Canine Companions for Independence trained Charger to do many tasks—including carrying Andrew's homework.*

▽ **HOSPITAL VISITOR** *Mirko, a rottweiler, gets a hug from patient Tawauna Dawkins, 5, of Columbia, South Carolina. Mirko works as a therapy dog at Richland Memorial Hospital, in Columbia. His visits brighten the long days for patients there.*

JOHN T. MILLER

THOMAS NEBBIA (ABOVE AND LEFT)

△ **HI, THERE!** *For people like Louise Leber, pets are good medicine. Heath, a Labrador, visits her retirement home regularly. The residents love to hold Heath and talk to him, says Paul Creed, of Hackettstown, New Jersey, who raised the dog.*

◁ ALL EARS. *Students line up during obedience training at Red Acre Farm Hearing Dog Center, in Stow, Massachusetts. These dogs will act as ears for the deaf, alerting their owners to such sounds as those of doorbells and smoke detectors.*

△ RISE AND SHINE. *Trainer Diane Mallett pats Tache after the dog signals that an alarm clock has sounded. After about three months at the center, Tache will move in with a deaf person. Waking her owner when the alarm rings will be an important part of Tache's job.*

27

(Continued from page 25) meals, keep their homes warm in winter, and get outside for exercise.

What makes a dog a good candidate for becoming a service dog for disabled people? First, it must have an even disposition. That means it doesn't chase cats or other dogs. It ignores loud noises and stays calm in crowds where people may accidentally jostle it or even kick it. For this reason, many service dog organizations train only breeds that have proved to be dependable working dogs. Canine Companions, for example, prefers Labrador retrievers, golden retrievers, German shepherds, and Doberman pinschers as service dogs. For hearing dogs, they use smaller breeds, such as Border collies and Welsh corgis. And for hospital and nursing home visitors, small dogs generally work well because they take up little space.

Although some breeds make better service dogs than others, breeding isn't everything. To grow up as a friendly, gentle animal that likes people and is willing to work closely with them, a dog needs a lot of care and affection as a puppy. The best source of this affection, dog guide organizations have discovered, is a child. All across the United States, children who belong to such groups as the 4-H Club, Girl Scouts, and Future Farmers of America volunteer as foster parents. The children and their families take the puppies into their homes for about a year. They teach the animals basic obedience and good manners, and help them feel comfortable around people. Then comes the hardest part of a puppy raiser's job: returning the dog to the organization that will train it to work with a blind or otherwise disabled person.

"It's hard to give up each puppy," says Tracy Farlow, 11, of San José, California. Tracy raises puppies for Guide Dogs for the (Continued on page 33)

◁ PUPPY LOVE. *Tracy Farlow, 11, of San José, California, holds a golden retriever. Tracy raises dog guides through the 4-H Club.*

THOM AINSWORTH, DIR. OF TRAINING, GUIDE DOGS FOR THE BLIND, INC.

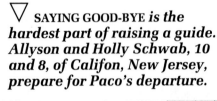

▽ SAYING GOOD-BYE *is the hardest part of raising a guide. Allyson and Holly Schwab, 10 and 8, of Califon, New Jersey, prepare for Paco's departure.*

◁ PUPPY RAISER *Rodney Giddens, 11, of Teaneck, New Jersey, hugs Bear. "Knowing he'll help a blind person makes me feel good," says Rodney.*

JOHN T. MILLER (LEFT, ABOVE, OPPOSITE)

▷ DOOLEY, REST! *Holly uses a hand signal to teach Dooley to sit and stay. Holly and her sister received Dooley when they returned Paco to The Seeing Eye.*

◁ **FUTURE GUIDES** *greet instructor Cathie Laber at the Guide Dogs for the Blind kennel, in San Rafael, California. The group trains golden retrievers, Labrador retrievers, and German shepherds—breeds that make especially good guides.*

△ IN HARNESS. *Rally, a German shepherd, takes his final exam at The Seeing Eye. The instructor works blindfolded while a supervisor judges the dog's work. Rally has learned to pull forward to lead his partner. Normally, dogs don't lead, they follow.*

(Continued from page 28) Blind, Inc., an organization based in California. Tracy has volunteered her time and her love to the future guides since she was 8. "You have to love the puppies to be a good trainer," she says. "If you don't love them, they won't make good dogs."

A number of organizations train dogs as guides for the blind. The oldest, and perhaps the best known, is The Seeing Eye, in Morristown, New Jersey. Founded in 1929, The Seeing Eye has trained more than 9,000 dogs and graduated more than 5,000 human partners.

At The Seeing Eye, dogs undergo several months of instruction before they meet their new owners. Instructors teach the dogs to stop at all curbs, to check for traffic before crossing streets, and to avoid obstacles. The dogs even learn to steer away from low awnings and branches that they could easily pass under, but that their owners might bump into.

Once a dog has completed its training, it is matched with a blind person. Then dog and partner spend a busy month training together. Under the supervision of an instructor, the pair travels in city traffic, boards buses and trains, and practices navigating in stores and restaurants. When the instructor thinks the partners are ready, they "solo," finding their way through downtown Morristown with the instructor watching—but not helping.

As Kristen Knouse, of Medford, New Jersey, and Ginger Torine, of Janesville, Wisconsin, learned, it's the blind person's responsibility to know the route to follow and to command the dog. It's the dog's job to guide its owner safely past obstacles and through traffic. When Kristen says "Shane, forward!" for example, her dog should start moving ahead. If a car is speeding toward them, however, Shane must ignore the order. The Seeing Eye instructors call this

◁ **CROSSING THE STREET** *in Morristown, New Jersey, is a big step for these girls and their new Seeing Eye dogs. Ginger Torine, of Janesville, Wisconsin, reaches the curb with her dog, Rhonda. Kristen Knouse, of Medford, New Jersey, and Shane cross after them.*

△ **A PASSING TRUCK** *tests Rhonda's ability to disobey. After Ginger told her dog to go forward, Rhonda waited until a truck that Ginger wasn't aware of had safely passed.*

▷ **ALL ABOARD.** *Shane waits as Kristen feels for a step at the Morristown train station.*

JOHN T. MILLER (ALL)

decision-making skill "intelligent disobedience."

After her month of training, Kristen began her senior year at high school—with Shane to guide her from class to class. Ginger, with her dog, Rhonda, entered college. The girls can expect their dogs to work for eight to ten years. Then the dogs will retire, and the girls will receive new partners. What happens to their faithful old partners? They may be adopted by a friend or a family member, or return to The Seeing Eye, where they will be retired or given to a loving family that will care for them.

If you see a blind person with a dog guide on the street, you may be tempted to pet it. Don't. When a dog guide is wearing its harness, it is working. Your friendly gesture might distract it from its duty, and cause possible injury to the dog's owner. Instead, you might speak to the blind person about the dog. People who own dog guides are proud of their partners, and are usually glad to tell others about them.

◁ GETTING CLOSE. *Learning to love and trust each other is a big part of the training for both Ginger and Rhonda.*

▽ ICE CREAM BREAK. *As their dogs rest at their feet, Ginger and Kristen enjoy a snack.*

DOGS
USING TEAMWORK

The wind howls. The temperature falls far below freezing. Snow swirls around, making it hard to see. The sky grows dark as the short winter day ends. But the loaded sled keeps going. The power moving it doesn't come from an engine. It comes from a team of dogs. The tough, densely furred animals, bred to survive the harsh arctic winter, are doing what they do best: pulling a sled.

Today, both native peoples and others who have settled in the far north most often rely on airplanes and snowmobiles to travel over the frozen landscape. Not long ago, however, the only way to go was by dogsled.

No one knows for certain where or when dogs were first hitched to sleds. Native peoples in northern parts of Europe and Asia may have used dogsleds many thousands of years ago. In North America, archaeologists have found evidence that people have used sled dogs for at least 1,500 years. Images of dogs and sleds are found on some ancient Eskimo carvings.

Sled dog teams played an important role

SLED DOG TEAMS *pad across the snow during an Eskimo seasonal migration. For centuries, sturdy dogs have served people in arctic regions. Before airplanes and snowmobiles reached the far north, the only way to travel was by dogsled.*

in the history of the far north. Native peoples used the teams to follow the migrating animals they hunted. Explorers used them. So did trappers looking for furs. Miners searching for gold during the Alaska gold rushes of the late 1800s relied on dogs to haul in supplies—and to haul out any gold they might find. The Royal Canadian Mounted Police depended on dog teams during their long winter patrols.

Dogsled mail delivery was at its peak in the early 1900s. In those days, the dogs pulled heavy sleds along a 2,000-mile system of trails that linked mining camps between Seward and Nome. As recently as 1963, winter mail was carried by sled.

Part of the Alaskan mail delivery route was called the Iditarod Trail. Iditarod comes from a word meaning "distant place" in an Eskimo language. In 1925, the strange name became a household word all over the world.

In January of that year, the isolated town of Nome, Alaska, was hit by an outbreak of diphtheria, which in those days was often a fatal illness. Many people's lives were threatened by the disease. Just one thing could save them: a supply of vaccine that was available only in Nenana, a town 674 miles away.

Today, 674 miles doesn't sound like a long way. But in the remote, frozen Alaska of 1925, the distance might as well have been 674,000 miles. The weather was so bad that airplanes could not be used to deliver the medicine. The solution: deliver the vaccine by dogsled.

Over the week beginning January 27, teams of drivers and their dogs relay-raced a package of diphtheria vaccine across some of the most rugged country on earth, through some of the worst winter weather. Part of the route followed the Iditarod Trail. The temperature fell to minus 64°F., and the sun shone for only a (Continued on page 43)

◁ HIKER'S HELPER. *Near his home, in Estes Park, Colorado, Christopher Thorp, 13, stows gear in the pack worn by Drifter, a golden retriever.*

▷ A MALAMUTE *fords a stream carrying 30 pounds of its owner's camera equipment.*

△ FLOWER POWER. *Pulling a flower cart is just for show for this Bernese mountain dog. Andy, a female, and Max, the larger male, work at winning championships at dog shows. In Switzerland, dogs like these still haul carts along steep mountain roads.*

◁ SUMMER EXERCISE. *To stay in shape for the winter racing season, Samoyeds work out by pulling a three-wheeled racing rig over the grass.*

▷ WINTER RACE. *Leslie Fields drives her team of Samoyeds in a race at Lake Dillon, Colorado. "This is near the start of the race. My team has just passed another Samoyed team," she reports. "They look very pleased with themselves."*

▽ GO FOR IT! *During a sprint in Fairbanks, Alaska, a mixed-breed husky gives its all. Booties protect its front paws from hard snow and sharp ice.*

◁ WINTER CARNIVAL *in Stowe, Vermont, draws teams like this one from all over New England and Canada. More than 40 states and all provinces have sled dog clubs. Races are held almost every weekend all winter long.*

(Continued from page 39) few hours each day.

In spite of the hardship, a driver and his team reached Nome at 5:30 a.m. on February 2. Nome was saved, thanks to the courage and toughness of 100 sled dogs and the men who drove them. The daring feat made headlines all over the world. People called it the "Race for Life."

Yelping and yowling, teams of sled dogs prepare to take off from the starting line. There are Alaskan and Siberian huskies, Samoyeds, malamutes, and Eskimo dogs. The mushers, drivers named from the French word *marcher* (mar-SHAY)— to walk, are ready to begin their thousand-mile trip.

The scene is Anchorage, Alaska. The event is the Iditarod Trail Sled Dog Race, a contest that has begun on the first Saturday in March since 1973. The race commemorates the 1925 "Race for Life" to save Nome from diphtheria.

The Iditarod is the World Series of dogsledding. At more than 1,100 miles, it is the longest sled dog race in the world, and the most challenging. Along the way from Anchorage to Nome, racers must struggle with rough terrain, with terrible weather, and with an occasional angry moose. The race can take from 11 days to more than 3 weeks to complete.

"The winner isn't who runs the dogs the most; it's who takes care of them the most," says one Iditarod racer. Along the trail, musher and dogs stop at about 25 checkpoints spaced from 30 to 90 miles apart. There, veterinarians check on the dogs as mushers give their teams food and water. During the race, the dogs may eat as often as 10 times a day. After a rest and a meal, the hardy dogs are ready to run again.

As Susan Butcher, winner of three straight Iditarods, says, "The dogs must have a love of running, and a never-say-die attitude."

Although the Iditarod   (Continued on page 46)

◁ **YOUNG MUSHER** *Kriya Dunlap, 12, of Bakers Mills, New York, thaws the brass snap of a dog line with her breath. Kriya has entered the Ninth Annual Alpo International Sled Dog Race, at Saranac Lake, New York. She has raced sled dogs since she was 3.*

▽ **GETTING READY.** *Kriya fastens the dog line to her sled before the race. Her three-dog team will be harnessed to the line. Kriya placed fifth in the event. She likes the excitement of racing. But more important, she says, is the love and respect she feels for her dogs.*

RANDA BISHOP (ALL)

△ **RACING PARTNERS.** *Kriya gives Castle, her lead dog, a hug. As lead, Castle sets the pace for the rest of the team. Kriya's family breeds and raises racing huskies.*

◁ A TEN-DOG TEAM *of huskies trots along a trail in Snowmass, Colorado. Their load: visitors enjoying the scenery. These dogs have a relatively easy life. Their ancestors were hardworking helpers for native peoples who lived and hunted in arctic regions.*

DAVID HISER (BOTH)

△ JUST 12 DAYS OLD, *these husky pups are barely a handful for Marion Winkler. In just a few weeks, they'll be strong enough to survive an arctic night outside. Winkler, of Krabloonik Kennel, in Snowmass, cares for and trains almost 300 sled dogs.*

(Continued from page 43) is the longest, toughest sled dog race, it is only one race among dozens that take place each weekend all through the winter.

Sled dog racing is a popular sport among young people as well as among adults. The International Sled Dog Racing Association, formed in 1966, recognizes 100 races a year. At many of these, spectators can watch as small children hitch sleds to a single dog for 100-yard "Kid and Mutt" races. Before long, these enthusiastic young mushers graduate to junior categories for more formal competition. They begin with 3-dog-team races for 12- to 17-year-olds, later working up to 6- and 8-dog runs.

Riding a dogsled isn't as easy as it looks. A musher must have good balance and be in top physical condition. Often, the driver leaps from the sled and runs alongside it as the dogs struggle over rough ground or make sharp turns.

There are no reins for steering a dogsled. Mushers communicate with their dogs by shouting commands. "Hut!" "Hike!" "All right!" or "Let's Go!" gets the dogs moving. "Gee!" means turn right, and "Haw!" means turn left. A loud "Whoa!" brings the team to a halt.

One thing a musher rarely has to do is persuade the team to start running. Iditarod winner Susan Butcher says of her dogs at the beginning of a race, "They're so eager to get going that it takes ten people to hold them."

Sled dogs are bred to be tough. They have to be, since they live in some of the harshest places on earth. Through the centuries, northern dogs have spent their lives outdoors, sleeping on the ice with their backs to the wind and their tails curled around their noses.

Descended from generations of northern dogs, today's sled dogs have heavy coats of dense fur and

© JEFF SCHULTZ 1988 (BOTH)

△ AT A CHECKPOINT *during the Iditarod Trail Sled Dog Race, in Alaska, huskies rest. They need the break. The race covers more than 1,100 miles.*

▷ IDITAROD CHAMPION *Susan Butcher shows off her lead dogs Granite, sitting up, and Sluggo. Susan won the demanding races of 1986, 1987, and 1988. When* *she's not racing, Susan and her husband live in an isolated cabin in Alaska and care for 150 sled dogs that they have raised and trained.*

strong, padded feet. They are excellent athletes, well adapted to an active life in the cold. Sled dogs would rather run in the cold than spend a cozy night in a heated kennel. The dogs are born with a strong urge to pull. Even before it's hitched to a sled, a five-month-old sled dog puppy can pull a car tire around the yard.

The pure sled dog breeds are the Siberian husky, the Alaskan malamute, and the Samoyed. Siberian huskies are medium-size dogs about two feet tall, weighing between 35 and 60 pounds. They're muscular, strong, and fast. Alaskan malamutes are large dogs that can pull sleds for long distances without tiring. About two feet tall, they weigh between 75 and 85 pounds. Samoyeds have pure white coats. Eskimo people once wove combings from the coats into yarn that they made into clothes. Samoyeds work well even in very cold weather. They have tough feet with protective (Continued on page 52)

△ BACK OFF! *A fearless Eskimo dog chases a polar bear away from its food. This dog lives in Churchill, Canada, a town invaded by polar bears for several weeks each year.*

▷ ON THE TRAIL *during a hunting expedition, an Eskimo untangles his dogs' lines. He is looking for seals on the sea ice off northwest Greenland.*

FLUFFY PUPPIES. *These Siberian husky pups will soon be old enough to try out a harness. That's no hardship. There's nothing a sled dog would rather do than pull and run. Trainers often hitch puppies with more experienced dogs to teach them teamwork. The pups think it's all a game.*
ART WOLFE/IMAGE BANK

(Continued from page 48) hair between the toes. "Sams" are compact dogs just under two feet tall, weighing about 35 to 70 pounds.

Mixed-breed sled dogs, known simply as Alaskan huskies, often make superior racers. The mixed breeds tend to be strong and fast. They are often found working on dogsled teams, and may run as fast as 25 miles an hour during short sprints.

Its special qualities make the sled dog an ideal helper for polar explorers. Robert Peary, who used dog teams on his historic arctic expeditions, said that without the dogs, "It would be folly to think of attempting the conquest of The Great Ice."

Japanese explorer Naomi Uemura used huskies during his solo trek to the North Pole in 1978. For two months, the dogs, which pulled a heavy sled loaded with the explorer's provisions, were his only companions as he struggled across the enormous, constantly moving blocks of ice that cover the Arctic Sea near the North Pole.

During his lonely, daring journey to the Pole, Uemura was occasionally resupplied by airplane. The planes took some of his dogs out when they became too tired to go on, and brought him fresh ones.

When American Will Steger led an eight-person expedition on a walk to the North Pole in 1986, the group decided to make the trip without any resupply. That meant they had to carry everything they would need on their dogsleds.

The expedition, made up of seven men and one woman, would be the first to reach the Pole without resupply since Robert Peary's controversial trip in 1909. Today, some people doubt that Peary ever reached the Pole. Team member Ann Bancroft would be the the first woman ever to walk to the North Pole. The expedition could not have succeeded without the support of the 49 dogs that went

IRA BLOCK (BELOW AND CENTER)

▷ GREENLAND TOUR. *Eleven dogsled teams cross sea ice near Angmagssalik Island, in Greenland. The people on the sleds are not scientists or professional explorers. They're sightseers out for adventure.*

△ ALONE ON THE ICE. *With only his huskies for company, Japanese explorer Naomi Uemura walks to the North Pole. At times, fresh dogs were flown in to replace those that had become tired.*

▷ I MADE IT! *On April 29, 1978, after crossing 500 miles of dangerous, shifting ice, Uemura reaches his goal. Afterward, he gave his faithful sled dogs victory hugs. He couldn't have made it without them.*

© GEORGE HOLTON, THE NATIONAL AUDUBON SOCIETY
COLLECTION/PHOTO RESEARCHERS (RIGHT)

along. The explorers used Canadian Eskimo dogs, known for endurance and resistance to cold, and huskies, known for speed.

The group carried their supplies on five heavy sleds weighed down with a lot of dog food. The dogs ate pemmican—a high-calorie, high-protein mixture of raw dried beef and fat. As the sled loads grew lighter over the eight-week journey, some of the dogs were airlifted out. Two injured members of the expedition also were airlifted to safety. By the time the team arrived at the Pole, on May 3, 1986, twenty dogs pulling two sleds accompanied the six explorers who remained.

When the adventurers returned after reaching the North Pole, they didn't forget their faithful dogs. They said, "We are deeply indebted to the huskies and Canadian Eskimo dogs that pulled so hard and long to bring us here to the top of the world. They are the real heroes of this journey."

◁ WE CAN DO IT. *A team strains to haul a sled over a ridge of ice during a 1986 expedition to the North Pole. The sled with its load weighed a thousand pounds—much of it dog food.*

▽ HUSKY HOWL. *En route to the Pole, a dog demands dinner.*

JIM BRANDENBURG

© H. MARK WEIDMAN

DOGS
KEEPING THE PEACE

Max, a German shepherd—and a canine law enforcement officer in the Orange County, Florida, sheriff's office—sails over a broad jump. He's not running the obstacle course for fun. It's part of his training at the Central Florida Criminal Justice Institute, in Orlando.

"The K-9 has to jump over, crawl through, or climb obstacles that might be encountered on the street," says Robert L. Cook, coordinator of K-9 (short for canine) training at the institute. When chasing a fleeing crime suspect, a law enforcement dog may have to scale a wall, climb a ladder, or leap across a deep ditch. If Max runs into such situations while he's on duty, he'll be prepared.

Training a dog for law enforcement work is serious business. The animal must be intelligent, strong, loyal, and obedient. It must know when to be fierce and when to be gentle. It must be brave enough to continue working even under gunfire.

Over the years, dogs have proved again and again that they have what it takes to protect people, catch criminals, and enforce the

BROAD JUMP. *At the Central Florida Criminal Justice Institute, in Orlando, a German shepherd named Max jumps a series of hurdles. Max is a police dog. This training keeps him in condition for street duty with his police officer partner.*

law. For this reason, police departments, military forces, airport security units, and the Secret Service, an agency whose duties include protecting the President and the President's family, rely on dogs to help them do their jobs.

Dogs have protected people and guarded property for centuries. Old records show that guard dogs worked in the dock areas of Saint-Malo, France, 600 years ago. In England, bloodhounds tracked down criminals as early as the 1600s. It wasn't until the 20th century, however, that dog-and-officer teams became a familiar sight.

In 1956, Baltimore, Maryland, organized the first K-9 program in the United States. The idea quickly spread across the country. Today, hundreds of communities depend on law enforcement dogs.

It's no wonder that dogs make perfect partners for police officers. The animals can do many things a human partner can't do. Their hearing is more acute than a human's. Their sense of smell is much better, too. They can run faster, go farther, and crawl into tighter places than a human can. These skills give a dog's human partner an advantage over criminals. The dog can sense the presence of a hidden suspect when its partner can't. And the dog will risk its own life to attack someone who is threatening its partner.

Sometimes, the mere presence of a trained police dog can keep a crime from taking place. A transit policeman in New York City recalls this experience: He and his canine partner were on a break from their job patrolling the subway system. Suddenly, a man with a large knife appeared and began slashing out at people walking by.

"Watch him," the officer ordered his dog. That command told the dog to focus on and stare at the suspect, ready to attack. Just a glance at the snarling dog was enough for the man with the knife. He

PETER R. HORNBY (LEFT)

© SALLY ANNE THOMPSON

◁ ON THE LOOKOUT, *Bart, a patrol dog with the New Hampshire police, watches the neighborhood. K-9s, or police dogs, have been on duty in New Hampshire for 25 years.*

△ STANDING GUARD *on a street in London, England, a police dog protects a suitcase full of camera equipment. Meanwhile, its police officer partner can attend to other duties.*

▽ MAKING FRIENDS. *At Forest Heights Elementary School, in Oxon Hill, Maryland, second graders get acquainted with a four-footed member of their local police force. K-9 representatives often visit schools to explain their work.*

DANIEL P. BEIGEL

immediately dropped his weapon and surrendered.

In this case, the dog didn't have to touch the man at all. If the man had continued to strike out with the knife, the police officer would have commanded, "Get him!" Then the dog would have leapt for the attacker's arm and held on until its human partner told it to let go.

If you visited a training center for law enforcement dogs, you'd probably notice right away that most of the students are German shepherds. Although other large breeds, including Doberman pinschers and rottweilers, sometimes work as K-9s, years of experience have shown that the German shepherd is the ideal dog for police work. It is large, strong, and intelligent. It has a powerful bite—700 pounds per square inch. It's also loyal, has a natural urge to protect people, and can work in almost any climate.

A K-9 training course usually lasts about three months. It begins with basic obedience. Dogs and handlers work together as the animals learn to respond to spoken commands and hand signals.

Handlers teach the dogs by repeating such commands as "stay," "come," and "heel," over and over. When a dog reacts correctly, it is rewarded with praise and petting. When it does the wrong thing, the handler does not praise it. Instead, he or she says "No," and may jerk firmly—but harmlessly—on the dog's leash.

The handler never hits the dog when it disobeys, but is always patient and in control. The goal of basic training is to create an obedient animal, not a mean one. During this time, a handler and dog begin to build a lifelong partnership based on trust and affection, not fear.

Once a K-9 has learned basic obedience, it moves on to agility drills. By learning to jump taller and taller hurdles, to scale (Continued on page 64)

THOMAS NEBBIA (ALL)

△ GET HER! *A padded sleeve protects a trainer's arm during an attack lesson at the Central Florida Criminal Justice Institute. The dog will learn to catch and hold a suspect on command—even under gunfire.*

▷ UP AND OVER. *Officer Lisa Bowen encourages Duke, her K-9 partner, as he runs an obstacle course. This training pays off when a dog has to leap fences or climb through windows during a chase.*

▷ HUG BREAK. *Between classes, Susan Ricchuito pets Karo, her partner and friend. Police and their dogs must develop a strong bond of trust. An officer's life may depend on the dog's loyalty and skill.*

▷ CHECK IT OUT! *In an airplane, detector dog Josh lets handler Mike Viena know there's something suspicious in a baggage compartment. Search specialists like Josh are trained to sniff out dangerous substances, such as explosives.*

THOMAS NEBBIA (BOTH)

△ SUBWAY SAFETY. *A young New York City subway rider meets a transit officer and his K-9 partner. The presence of the dogs in the city's huge underground rail system reassures law-abiding riders and discourages criminals.*

(Continued from page 60) walls, to climb ladders, and to leap from moving cars, the dog becomes a strong, skilled athlete. Then it is ready to begin training in attacking, searching, and tracking.

During attack training, a K-9 learns to bite and hold a suspect—and to let go immediately when its partner tells it to. The dog must know how to use its own judgment at times. The police dog is trained not to attack unless it is commanded to by its partner—with one exception. If the partner's safety is threatened—if a suspect knocks down or shoots at an officer, for example—the dog will attack on its own. Police officers' lives have been saved by the ability of dogs to act on their own in such situations.

During search training, the K-9 learns to find people hidden inside buildings. It also sharpens its ability to find objects concealed outdoors. It can locate stolen wallets or sniff out guns that have been thrown away after a crime. The dog also is taught to track—follow a scent trail to find someone who has run away or become lost.

When a K-9's training is complete, it is ready to help its partner patrol the streets on foot or in a squad car. It is prepared to keep order in crowds, chase suspects, and catch criminals. Always alert, the dog may attack and disarm a robbery suspect in the morning and respond to the petting and hugs of a passing child in the afternoon.

Law enforcement dogs do help keep the peace. Police departments report that where K-9s are used, their value can't even be measured. A typical K-9 will work for a police force for about six years—identified by a badge, just as its partner is. In its free time, it will live with its partner's family as a pet.

After some dogs have completed their basic training, they go through even more specialized training. They become four-footed detectives,

PAM SMITH O'HARA (BELOW AND LEFT)
THOMAS NEBBIA (RIGHT)

▽ **DETECTOR DOG** *Jon Henry sits to signal that he smells fruit hidden in a suitcase by U. S. Department of Agriculture K-9 officer David Brannaka.*

▽ **A TREAT** *for each job well done encourages Jon Henry to keep working hard.*

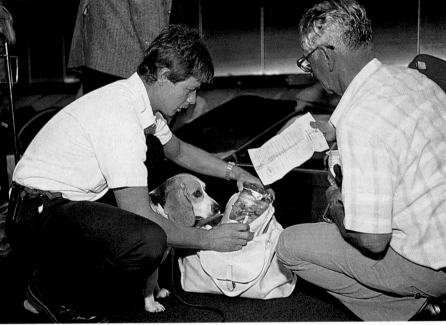

△ **FORBIDDEN FOOD** *is handed over at an airport. This man turned in food he had bought in a foreign country. If he had hidden it, Jon Henry would have sniffed it out. Keeping certain products out of the United States protects crops and livestock from disease.*

▷ **HER GREEN COAT** *identifies Lady as a member of the U. S. Department of Agriculture's Beagle Brigade. The brigade's beagles are trained to recognize the smell of beef, pork, and more than 30 other foods. The dogs work at international airports around the country.*

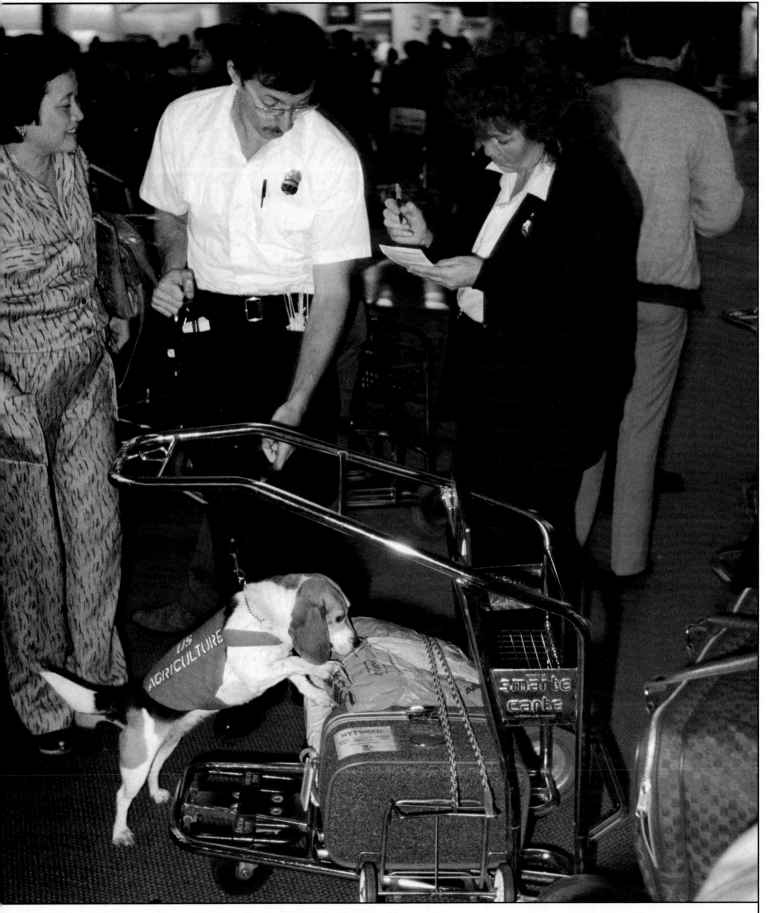

sniffing out the explosives used to make bombs or the ingredients in illegal drugs. Some detector dogs learn to identify substances that cause pollution. Others sniff out leaks in underground natural gas pipelines. Still others are trained to locate forbidden agricultural products hidden in luggage that enters the United States from other countries. Such products might contain insects or diseases that could harm American livestock or crops.

Some of the most highly skilled dogs of all receive their training at Lackland Air Force Base, at San Antonio, Texas. There, the U. S. Department of Defense runs a dog-training unit that prepares all the dogs that work with the different branches of the U. S. military. The trainers at Lackland also prepare animals for work as police dogs, bomb detector dogs, and Secret Service dogs. Today, more than 2,000 Lackland canine graduates are on duty, protecting our nation's interests all over the world.

◁ ON PATROL *at Lackland Air Force Base, at San Antonio, Texas, a German shepherd and its handler pass a row of jet fighters during their turn on guard duty.*

▽ CORPS MASCOT. *English bulldogs like TJ have symbolized the U. S. Marine Corps since World War I.*

RANDA BISHOP

THOMAS NEBBIA

DOGS
FINDING THE LOST

S kiers love the thrill of riding a chair lift to the top of a snowy run. They look forward to zipping back down the mountain. Skiing is fun!

But the deep snow and steep slopes that make skiing enjoyable may also add up to danger. Sometimes large blocks of snow break off mountainsides and crash downhill. The wall of snow, known as an avalanche, buries everything in its path.

Avalanches zoom downhill faster than even the best skier can go. The falling snowpack may reach 200 miles an hour. About 100,000 avalanches occur in the mountains of the western United States each year.

If avalanches bury people, the victims must be found and dug out quickly, before they suffocate. In the Rocky Mountains, for example, a victim buried by an avalanche must be rescued within 30 minutes to survive. That's where specially trained dogs such as Chopper come in. That's Chopper riding the chair lift in the photograph at the right. He is a member of the Ski Patrol at Aspen, a mountain resort in the Colorado

GETTING A LIFT TO WORK. *Chopper, a search-and-rescue (SAR) dog, accompanies a ski patrol to the slopes of Aspen, a Colorado resort. Chopper, a golden Labrador retriever, is trained to sniff out people buried by avalanches.*

Rockies. Chopper uses his keen sense of smell to find people buried by avalanches.

Rescue workers use search dogs to help them after avalanches, earthquakes, and other disasters. Dogs also help find backpackers and hunters who have become lost in the wilderness, and even people who have simply wandered away from home and can't find the way back. The hardworking search-and-rescue, or SAR, dogs are experts at locating people by the scent they give off.

If you have a dog, you know that it sometimes sniffs you over when you get home. The smell clinging to your clothing tells the dog whether you've walked in the woods, taken a rest in a meadow, or stopped to pet another dog. Dogs recognize other dogs—and people—by scent.

Dogs can follow a human scent trail because each person gives off his or her own odor. The odor comes from cell particles that constantly fall from the body. Every day, a human body sheds and replaces about 50 million dead skin and hair cells. The particles fall even if the person is standing still.

Most of the cell particles people shed are too small to be seen without a microscope—but they're there. Tiny organisms feed on the dead cells. As they eat the cells, the organisms release a faint odor. We usually can't smell it, but a dog can. That odor, combined with perspiration and oil from the body—and any perfume, cosmetics, or soap the person uses—add up to a special "signature" smell.

Everyone's signature smell is different, just as distinctive as a fingerprint. When you walk across a room or through the woods, you leave an invisible trail of your signature smell in the air behind you. It also settles on the ground around your feet and is left around your footprints.

A search-and-rescue (Continued on page 74)

◁ GO, BEAR! *Dr. Janet Brennan sends Bear, her German shepherd, on a practice search in Yosemite National Park, in California. Bear is part of the California Rescue Dog Association, an organization of dogs and handlers that find people lost in the wilderness.*

▽ IN YOSEMITE, *handlers check a map as their canine partners await the signal to start searching. These rescue dogs find missing people by smelling the air. When they detect the odor of a human, they follow the invisible scent trail to the lost person.*

△ TAKING A BREAK. *Toby rests in "his" station wagon after a search-and-rescue session. It takes a strong animal with a keen sense of smell to be an SAR dog.*

DAVID FALCONER (ALL)

◁ WATER RESCUE. *Logan greets a diver at the end of a training session in Colorado. His handler, mountain ranger Ann Wichman, praises her dog. Logan found the diver by smell, even though the man was deep below the surface of the lake.*

△ TAKE A WHIFF. *A German shepherd smells a "scent article" in a plastic bag. The dog will sniff for the unique odor of the person who left the article behind.*

▽ A BLOODHOUND, *a member of the New Hampshire police force, sits patiently as his handler adjusts his harness.*

(Continued from page 71) dog can sniff out and follow that trail. The scent trail fades with time, and changing winds and weather conditions can weaken it. A dog with a sensitive nose, however, can follow the trail many hours after it is laid down.

Dogs' noses are remarkably sensitive. Scientists can't even make machines that identify different odors as well as a canine nose can. The secret is in the dog's olfactory cells—cells that recognize scent chemicals in the air. Dogs have many more olfactory cells in their nasal passages than people do. A larger part of the canine brain is devoted to smell, too. A bloodhound—the champion of canine sniffers—has a sense of smell more than two million times more powerful than a human's. Some people call the bloodhound a "walking nose."

Police departments often rely on the bloodhound to find missing people. The dog is given a "scent article" to sniff to identify the person's signature smell. The article may be clothing the person wore or a sheet from a bed the person slept in. After it has a good whiff of the scent article, the bloodhound begins sniffing the ground. Once it finds the smell, it's off.

A bloodhound tracking a smell is a single-minded animal. Handlers report that the dog can become so absorbed in following the scent trail that it may run into a tree or a parked car. A handler follows the dog, holding a leash attached to its harness. The handler keeps the dog from hurting itself as it rushes after a scent. Once the bloodhound makes the find—tracks down the target—the dog relaxes. It may cover the object of the search with wet, sloppy kisses. Bloodhounds are gentle and friendly.

Because bloodhounds have such a keen sense of smell, some courts of law even accept as evidence the bloodhound's (Continued on page 78)

ANIMALS ANIMALS/ROBERT PEARCY

△ LOYAL MASCOT *of the fire company in Penryn, California, a Dalmatian looks right at home on a fire truck. In the 1890s, the dogs ran to fires beside horse-drawn engines, helping to keep the route clear. Today, they're kept as pets in many firehouses.*

▷ ON THE WAY UP. *Téo, a member of the fire department in Paris, France, climbs a ladder. Téo is trained to search for trapped people. He was flown in to aid in the search for victims after earthquakes in Mexico and El Salvador.*

▷ GETTING A LIFT. *A French fireman carries a German shepherd on his back to protect the animal's feet from broken glass or from hot surfaces at the scene of a fire. The dog's job is to search for any victims who may be left in the area.*

© BRIAN R. WOLFE, 1986 (BELOW AND RIGHT)

◁ A DOG *teams up with rescue workers to search for survivors after a 1986 earthquake in El Salvador that destroyed large buildings and took many lives. Dogs did find some people still alive in the ruins.*

△ AVALANCHE AID. *Rescue team members work at Alpine Meadows, a ski area in California, where a wall of rushing snow destroyed a building and killed seven people in 1982. One woman was found alive—thanks to an SAR dog named Bridget.*

(Continued from page 74) trail from a crime scene to a suspect. Other breeds also are good at finding missing people by following their scent trail. Beagles and Labrador retrievers, as well as many other pure and mixed breeds, make excellent trackers.

While many search-and-rescue dogs track individuals by following the scent they leave behind on the ground, other SAR dogs don't rely on scent articles. They get their clues by sniffing the air for the scent of missing people. Air-scenting dogs sniff all around an area where someone has disappeared, and then follow any human smell.

As they work, air-scenting dogs zigzag back and forth, covering a large area quickly. They work without leashes. Their handlers learn to tell by their behavior when the dogs are onto something. Some dogs may wag their tails. Others may prick up their ears or sit down. During training, a handler learns to recognize a dog's individual body language.

Air-scenting is an effective method of finding people after earthquakes, floods, and avalanches. The dogs smell human scent floating up through rubble or snow, and alert their handlers. Then rescue workers can dig out the disaster victims.

Search-and-rescue dogs work in units with other dogs and handlers. The units may include tracking dogs that follow a specific scent on the ground, and air-scenting dogs that sniff out evidence of any human presence. The National Association of Search and Rescue Dogs (NASAR), based in Fairfax, Virginia, counts among its members 72 independent SAR dog units in the United States.

When help is needed, SAR units will go anywhere. The U. S. Air Force provides air transportation when the search site can't be reached quickly any other way. In 1985, for example, 11 SAR dogs

STEVEN GOLDSTEIN PHOTOGRAPHY, INC.

DAVID CUPP (RIGHT)

▷ **CHAMP AND BUDDY** *saved Marvin Dacar when a tire weighing more than a ton fell on him. The dogs were out for a late-night run when they heard Dacar shouting for help. They barked until their owners came to the rescue.*

NOEL NEUBURGER

△ **QUICK ACTION** *helped Frankie, a sheepdog, save Mari Marks when a horse she was training nearly trampled her. The dog leapt into the horse's path and herded it away from the woman. Then Frankie ran to get help from a nearby stable.*

▷ **LIFESAVING PAL.** *In a California hospital, Anna Conrad plays with Bridget, the dog that found her after the avalanche at Alpine Meadows. Anna was trapped for five days. When Bridget located her and alerted rescuers, she became the first dog in North America to save an avalanche victim.*

were airlifted to Mexico City to help search for survivors of a devastating earthquake. Dogs from France and Switzerland were also flown in to help in the rescue effort.

Each SAR unit is a well-trained emergency team. When the dogs and their handlers go out to search for lost people or to assist after a disaster, they are equipped to stay out for three to five days. They bring camping gear, food, and medical supplies. The handlers are trained in emergency medical procedures, and know how to handle emergencies such as hypothermia. Hypothermia is a dangerous lowering of the body temperature often experienced by people who have been exposed to cold too long. Radios keep the teams in touch with a base camp.

The dogs and people work quickly and efficiently, and often save lives. The people who join such units are volunteers. Their reward for their hard, dangerous work is the satisfaction of knowing that

△ **SAINT BERNARDS** *love snow. It's a good thing! For hundreds of years, they saved people who had become lost in it. The dogs didn't really carry brandy in casks around their necks. That legend began when an English portrait artist gave a dog a keg in a painting.*

▷ **FIRST FLIGHT** *is a scary experience for a rescue dog in Park City, Utah. Practice sessions like this one accustom dogs to the noisy aircraft.*

they have saved lives that would otherwise be lost.

Bridget, a German shepherd, was a member of Wilderness Finders, a California search-and-rescue team nicknamed WOOF. The WOOF unit was called to the scene of an avalanche in Alpine Meadows, California, in March 1982. The dog made history when she found Anna Conrad. Anna was buried under more than ten feet of snow, inside the ruins of a building that the avalanche had smashed to bits. Some wooden lockers above her had kept the snow off her, and clothing from the lockers had enabled her to stay warm. It was the first time that a search-and-rescue dog in North America had found a living avalanche victim. Anna Conrad, who had been buried for five days, was the only survivor. Seven other people died in the avalanche.

When Bridget was taken to the area, she quickly alerted her handler to the presence of someone under the snow. Rescuers were excited and began to dig. They heard Anna call, "I'm OK. I'm alive!" Bridget was excited, too. As Anna was pulled from the snow, the dog grabbed a scrap of wood and tossed it into the air with joy. Later, Bridget was taken to the hospital to visit the young woman whose life she had saved.

SAR dogs are true heroes. They also are highly trained professionals. But even untrained dogs can save lives. Each year, the Ken-L Ration dog food company elects a national "dog hero" from among the millions of pet dogs Americans own. Hundreds of dogs are nominated for the award each year. A public vote decides the winner.

"Ken-L Ration has made a tradition of recognizing dogs who go above and beyond the call of duty," says George Yapp, who represents the company. Champ, a cairn terrier, and Buddy, a poodle and sheepdog mix, did just that when they saved a man

DAVID HISER

△ SUITED UP *in Aspen, Colorado, Chopper is ready for a day's training. The Labrador wears a red harness with a pouch containing a rescue beacon. That way, if Chopper should be buried in snow, his partners could follow his radio signal and quickly dig him out.*

▽ TAIL WAGGING, *Chopper starts digging for a hidden "victim," encouraged by ski patrollers Patty Edmondson and Rob Baxter. It takes Chopper about a minute to locate the buried person and start digging.*

▷ THERE YOU ARE! *His nose covered with snow, Chopper peers into a hollow to check on his find. Patty and Rob take a look, too. The avalanche rescue dog's reward for his successful search will be to play a game of tug-of-war with the "victim."*

DAVID HISER AND ANDREA BOOHER

DAVID HISER (RIGHT)

who was pinned under a heavy tire. Their quick action won both of them the 1986 Dog Hero title.

It was a cold night in Dickinson, North Dakota. Champ and Buddy had been let out for a late-night run. While they were out, they heard a man shouting for help. Marvin Dacar had been alone in a warehouse unloading freight when a tire weighing more than a ton fell on him, pinning him down. He called and called, but no one came. Then the dogs heard him. They alerted their owners, who telephoned the rescue squad. If Champ and Buddy hadn't come by, Marvin Dacar probably would have frozen to death in the below-zero North Dakota night.

There are hundreds of stories like that of Champ and Buddy. Dogs have helped their owners escape from burning buildings. They have pulled drowning people from rivers, lakes, and the ocean. When people are in trouble, they're in luck if there's an alert, intelligent dog nearby to come to the rescue.

◁ **THE NEWFOUNDLAND** *feels at home in the water. A powerful swimmer, it makes a good lifeguard. This "Newf" is taking its Water Rescue Dog exam in Wareham, Massachusetts. It must pass six swimming and obedience tests to be certified.*

▽ TO THE RESCUE! *A Newf doesn't hesitate when someone's in trouble. During a test, this dog leaps from a dock to save its "drowning" mistress.*

THOMAS NEBBIA (BOTH)

DOGS
STEALING THE SHOW

During a hunting expedition, a dog runs across a field. Suddenly, it stops and stands absolutely motionless in the tall grass. Its whole body is tense and still. It bends one leg, stretches its neck forward, stiffens its tail, and stares straight ahead—every sense alert. A bird must be hiding in the nearby underbrush.

The dog, a pointer, is showing the behavior that gives the breed its name. For hundreds of years, people have raised pointers to chase small game and to use their bodies to signal the location of birds or other animals. Graceful, energetic, and strong, pointers are excellent sporting dogs. They make good pets, too, so long as they get plenty of exercise. Field trials offer pointer owners who aren't hunters a chance to show off their dogs. Field trials are obedience competitions that test the skills the dogs are bred for.

Over the centuries, people have bred hundreds of different types of dogs to perform special tasks or to act in certain ways. Pointers already know their job when they are just puppies. A two-month-old pup that still is

PERFECT FORM. *A purebred English pointer shows off the form that gave the breed its name. When a pointer scents game, it stands completely still, bends one leg, extends its tail, and stares at prey to show a hunter where to find it.*

wobbly on its feet will cock one leg and point at butterflies or at other creatures it sees.

Today, there are more than a hundred distinct dog breeds. The American Kennel Club (AKC) recognizes 130 of them and divides them into seven groups. There are sporting dogs and hounds, working dogs and terriers, toy dogs and herding dogs. For purebred dogs that don't fit into these groups, there is the nonsporting category.

The AKC has established standards for each breed that describe exactly how various dogs should look. Breed standards establish what size and shape a dog should be, what kind of tail it should have, what its markings should look like, and what texture its coat should have. There also are standards for a dog's gait—the way it moves—and its temperament—how it responds to things around it.

At official AKC dog shows, individual dogs are judged on how close they come to the standards.

The club certifies about 2,500 dog shows each year. Many lively, though unofficial, competitions are held, too. Dog owners enjoy showing off their pets, whether they're champion poodles or lovable mutts.

"Tallyho!" an official shouts. At that signal, handlers release three eager dogs from their slip leads, or harnesses. The dogs almost fly off the starting line. They are taking part in a lure course.

Lure coursing, or lure chasing, is a sport for dogs, although people enjoy it, too. Designed to test the skills of a group of breeds called sighthounds, lure coursing involves chasing a plastic lure pulled across a large field. Lure coursing has all the excitement of hunting for live game—and the dogs don't seem to mind that their quarry is only a white plastic bag attached to a cord.

Sighthounds are special dogs. Centuries ago, they were bred to chase swift (Continued on page 93)

◁ FOLLOWING HIS NOSE, *Ben closes in on his prey, a stuffed pheasant. The photographer placed lights on the bird and on Ben's collar to capture the action. The yellow line shows the path the bird was pulled along. The red is Ben's route.*

▽ RETURN TRIP. *A golden retriever demonstrates its skill at a field trial in Gloucester, in England. Sporting dogs like this one were bred to pick up downed game and carry it to hunters. This dog carries a dummy, not an actual bird.*

PRISCILLA CONNELL: PHOTO/NATS

LOUIE PSIHOYOS/WOODFIN CAMP & ASSOCIATES (LEFT)

© R. WILLBIE

△ A LEAPING LAB *dives for dummy "game" that has been tossed into the water during a competition in Ohio. Labrador retrievers love water, and are fast, powerful swimmers. This dog will swim to the dummy and bring it to shore in no time.*

▽ THEY'RE OFF! *Kelly Kalibat, 16, left, and Kerynn Fisher, 15, "slip," or release, their basenjis during a practice run for a lure course race in a Washington, D. C., park. The basenjis, dogs of African origin, wear harnesses that slip off easily.*

PATRICIA FISHER (ALL)

△ A GRACEFUL AFGHAN *glides after a lure during a race in Maryland. Afghans are skilled sporting dogs from Afghanistan. They were bred to chase down prey in mountainous regions.*

▷ TUG-OF-WAR. *At the end of a race, a basenji happily tears at the "prey" it has been chasing—a white plastic bag. Lure coursing helps dogs stay in shape.*

(Continued from page 89) animals across open areas such as the deserts of Egypt and the barren mountainsides of Afghanistan. Such breeds as Afghan hounds, basenjis, borzois, Ibizan hounds, greyhounds, Irish wolfhounds, pharaoh hounds, salukis, Scottish deerhounds, and whippets all are sighthounds. Each of these breeds depends more on its keen eyesight than on its sense of smell to catch prey. In addition, each is a fast runner.

For a lure course race, a length of nylon cord is strung through pulleys set close to the ground. The course can include sharp angles, rounded curves, or a straightaway pattern across a large, open field. The pattern must be at least 500 yards long. Once the dogs are off, the line is reeled in mechanically so that the bouncing lure stays just out of the animals' reach. The dogs leap and twist in midair as they pursue the lure along its route. They run fast—up to 40 miles an hour. At the end of the course, the handlers finally let the dogs catch the lure. The racers grab it and shake it wildly.

The American Sighthound Field Association runs about 300 official lure course races each year. Judges choose winners on the basis of speed, enthusiasm, agility, endurance, and ability to follow the zigzagging lure. Lure coursing is a demanding sport, but sighthounds perform it well. That shouldn't be surprising when you consider that these breeds have been hunting for thousands of years. On the walls of Egyptian tombs dating from 2900 B.C., archaeologists have found scenes showing dogs that look like the sighthounds of today.

For dog owners, competitions such as shows, field trials, and lure courses are fun. People who don't own dogs can enjoy the animals, too. They can simply open a magazine, turn on the television, or go to a movie (Continued on page 96)

◁ LATEST LASSIE. *The seventh dog to play Lassie acts the star with Weatherwax. Viewers have loved Lassie since 1941, when the first movie about the brave collie appeared. The last six Lassies have been males.*

◁ OUR FAVORITE SHOW. *Josie, in front, and O.J., two canine actors, seem to be watching TV. They actually are looking at Bob Weatherwax, their owner, at* *his home in California. Weatherwax owns 25 dogs— and they're all pros. Perhaps the most famous is Lassie, on the TV screen.*

△ SUPERSTAR *Benji, shown with Zax, a robot in a 1984 TV series, has won two Georgie Awards, naming him Top Animal Entertainer of the Year.*

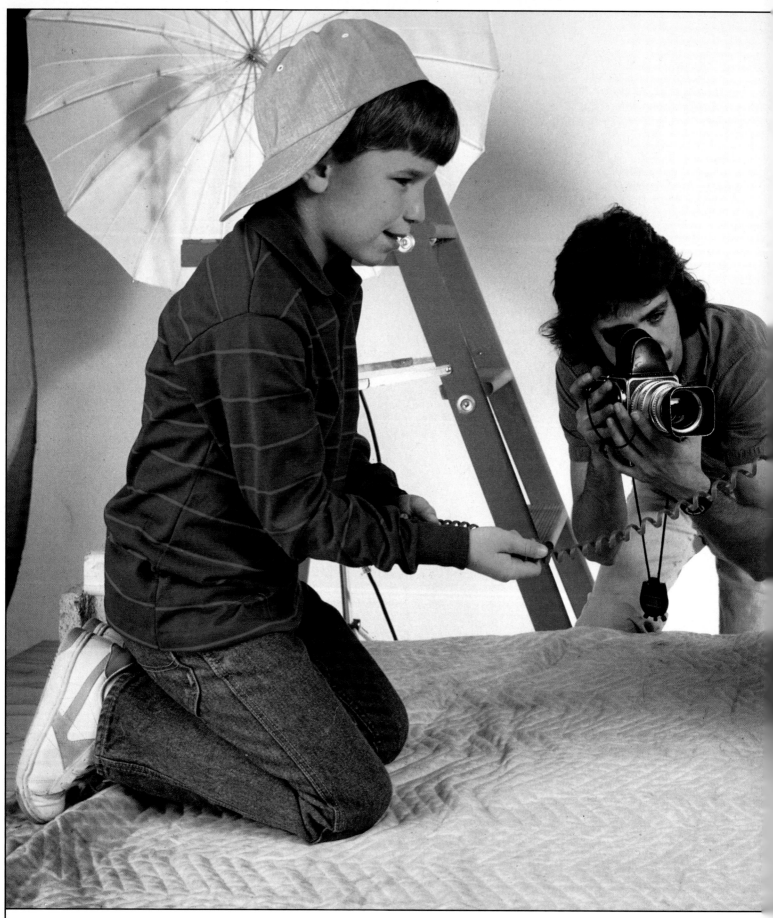

▽ RED RIBBON *decks the coat of a standard poodle named Andy-Dandie's Affair. This dog won the championship title at a show in Rio Linda, California. Poodles are among the most popular purebred dogs kept as pets in the United States.*

◁ IT'S FOR YOU. *Grumbles, a lovable and well-paid mutt, models for a television company advertisement. Working with him is Jason Failla, 9, of Fairfield, New Jersey. For a two-hour modeling session, an appealing dog model like Grumbles may receive $175, or even more.*

(Continued from page 93) or to the circus. When it comes to entertainment, dogs have been stealing the show for years.

Rin Tin Tin, one of the most famous entertainment dogs of all time, began life near a French airfield during World War I. A soldier adopted the German shepherd pup, took him home, and trained him to do stunts. The dog appeared in his first silent movie in 1923, and quickly became a star. There were many more Rin Tin Tin films, starring first the original Rin Tin Tin, and later his son and his grandson. A hit television show followed, which ran for five years.

Lassie, another famous canine movie star, first appeared in a film in 1941. But the collie's real fame came from the long-running TV adventure show "Lassie." The show aired every Sunday night for 18 years, beginning in 1953. Seven generations of collies played the brave Lassie. You may still be able to find reruns of the Lassie TV shows and movies.

Dog performers have powerful appeal today. They're also big money earners. Benji, the lovable "dog-next-door" superstar, has earned millions of dollars. Benji's very first movie earned 45 million dollars—not bad for an orphan mutt whose owner adopted him from the Humane Society in Burbank, California. A recent film, "Benji the Hunted," starring the son of the original Benji, made 22 million dollars during the summer of 1987.

What makes Benji so special? When Joe Camp, a Hollywood moviemaker, was searching for a dog to appear in a film, he wanted an animal that could "express genuine, honest emotion, show anxiety, fear, happiness, warmth, and love—a dog that could literally act." In shaggy, sweet-looking Benji, Joe Camp found the star he was looking for.

If you're concerned that dog actors may not get to have fun or live normal lives as pets, you can stop

RANDA BISHOP (ALL)

▷ TAKE A BOW. *At a class for dog performers in New York City, Grumbles and his owner, Lynne Witkin, demonstrate the proper response to applause. Lynne Witkin makes her living training dog performers and working with Grumbles and her other stunt dogs.*

△ HERE'S A HOOP. *Smiley Sam, a clown, teaches his Chihuahua a new trick. Lynne Witkin encourages the little dog to jump through the hoop.*

▷ SMILEY SAM *the clown and his partner, Giggles the Chihuahua, perform at parties for children in New York City. "Giggles has given enjoyment to kids of all ages," says Smiley Sam. "She's the kind of dog that responds well to everyone—and they, in turn, fall in love with her."*

worrying. At the end of the day, Benji and other professional animals like him go home with their owners to spend the evening as any other pet would. Also, the American Humane Association sends an observer to stay on the set of any movie that involves animals. The observer is there to make sure dogs and other performing creatures are not mistreated or endangered by their work.

Some professional dogs work as models for magazine and television advertisements. Like human actors and models, the animals are represented by agents who find them work.

Being a dog entertainer isn't easy. The animals must be highly trained. They learn to respond to many different hand signals from their owners or handlers, who stand in the background during photo sessions showing the animals what to do.

Sometimes, people have to come up with ideas to encourage the dogs. For one ad, for example, a photographer wanted a dog to act as though it were using a pay telephone in a booth. To get the dog to stand on its hind legs and reach for the phone, the photographer smeared the receiver with liverwurst. That did the trick.

When you watch a dog performing in a movie or laugh at the antics of a puppy on a TV commercial, you're enjoying the real pros of the entertainment-dog business. But amateur dogs can offer a lot of laughs, too. If you've ever played Frisbee with your dog, you know how much fun that can be.

Some organizations offer young dog owners the chance to perform with their dogs. In Columbia, Missouri, young people from 8 to 18 can enroll in the 4-H Dog Drill Team. All they need is a dog and some dedication. Members of the drill team enroll in the 4-H Club's dog care program. They study

◁ **POODLE PIROUETTE.** *Neecha Braun, 9, pairs up with a poodle during a circus performance in Miami, Florida.*

▷ **A SQUARE DANCE** *keeps members of the 4-H Dog Drill Team of Columbia, Missouri, on their toes. Their dogs sit in a neat row behind them.*

▽ **SHOW STOPPER.** *Gabby, a Brittany spaniel, breaks ranks to kiss Robby Young, 13, during a drill team performance.*

THOMAS NEBBIA

THOMAS NEBBIA (LEFT)

JAMES VANHOOSE (ABOVE AND BELOW)

△ **FRISBEE CHAMP** *Wizard does his stuff in Washington, D. C. The dog leapt from owner Peter Bloeme's thigh to catch the flying plastic disk.*

canine anatomy and learn how to identify different breeds. They practice showmanship and learn the rules the AKC has established for dog shows.

The drill team puts on shows in which the dogs and their owners perform tricks, square dances, and marches. The drill team has performed at state fairs, schools, retirement homes, and hospitals. Team members take the dogs visiting, too. Drill team members and dogs belong to Therapy Dogs International, a group dedicated to bringing the joy of dogs to people who cannot own pets of their own.

Over the years, the dog has proved its loyalty and its courage many times over. It has guarded our possessions and our safety. It has acted as our ears and our eyes. It has helped us reach the ends of the earth. And for all that it gives, the dog asks only love in return. If you were looking for a best friend, where could you find a better one?

◁ UP AND OVER. *Anita, a greyhound, clears a hurdle. The sleek racer went through her paces between events at a California rodeo.*

▽ THAT'S ALL, FOLKS. *At the end of a show, a Dalmatian performer named Buck gives his audience the last word.*

MISSION CITY AUTO LEASING & SALES

INDEX

Bold type indicates illustrations; regular type refers to text.

ADDITIONAL READING

Readers may want to check the *National Geographic Index* in a school or public library for related articles and to refer to the following books: *The AKC Complete Dog Book*, 17th edition, Howell Book House, Inc., 1987. Braund, Kathryn, *The Uncommon Dog Breeds*, Arco Publishing Co., Inc., 1975. Brown, Beth, *Dogs That Work For a Living*, Funk & Wagnalls, 1970. Bryson, Sandy, *Search Dog Training*, Boxwood, 1984. Emert, Phyllis Raybin, *Guide Dogs*, Crestwood House, 1985. Emert, Phyllis Raybin, *Hearing-Ear Dogs*, Crestwood House, 1985. Emert, Phyllis Raybin, *Sled Dogs*, Crestwood House, l985. Emert, Phyllis Raybin, *Law Enforcement Dogs*, Crestwood House, 1985. Emert, Phyllis Raybin, *Military Dogs*, Crestwood House, 1985. Emert, Phyllis Raybin, *Search and Rescue Dogs*, Crestwood House, l985. Glover, Harry, *A Standard Guide to Purebred Dogs*, McGraw-Hill, 1977. Leder, Jane Mersky, *Stunt Dogs*, Crestwood House, 1985. Longton, Tim and Edward Hard, *The Sheep Dog: Its Work and Training*, David & Charles, 1976. McPhee, Richard. *Tom & Bear: The Training of a Guide Dog Team*, Crowell 1981. Pearsall, Milo and Hugo Verbruggen, M. D., *Scent—Training to Track, Search, and Rescue*, Alpine Publications, Inc., 1982. Schwartz, Charlotte, *Friend to Friend, Dogs That Help Mankind*, Howell Book House, 1984. Silverstein, Alvin and Virginia, *Dogs, All About Them*, Lothrop, Lee & Shepard Books, 1986. Siegal, Mordecai, and Matthew Margolis, *Good Dog, Bad Dog*, New American Library, 1973. Siegel, Mary-Ellen and Hermine M. Koplin. *More Than a Friend: Dogs with a Purpose*, Walker and Co., 1984. Smith, Elizabeth Simpson, *A Guide Dog Goes to School*, William Morrow and Company, 1987. Taggart, Mari, *Sheepdog Training: An All Breed Approach*, Alpine Publications, Inc., 1986. *Alaska Geographic*, "Dogs of the North," Vol. 14, No. 1, 1987.

For more information about some of the organizations mentioned in this book, you may write to them at the addresses listed below.

The Seeing Eye
Washington Valley Road
Morristown, New Jersey 07960
Guide Dogs for the Blind, Inc.
P. O. Box 1200
San Rafael, California 94915
Canine Companions for Independence
P. O. Box 446
Santa Rosa, California 95402-0446
National Association of Search and Rescue Dogs (NASAR)
P. O. Box 3709
Fairfax, Virginia 22038
Red Acre Farm Hearing Dog Center
P. O. Box 278
Stow, Massachusetts 01775
4-H Clubs
Check with your local chapter.

CONSULTANTS

Bonnie V. G. Beaver, D.V.M., Texas A & M University—*Chief Consultant*

Barbara Wood, M.Ed.—*Reading Consultant*

Nicholas J. Long, Ph.D.—*Consulting Psychologist*

The Special Publications and School Services Division is grateful to the individuals named or quoted within the text and to those cited here for their generous assistance:

Bonnie Aikman, U.S. Department of Agriculture; Janet Brennan, Soquel, California; Robert L. Cook, Central Florida Criminal Justice Institute; Lorna Coppinger, Livestock Dog Project, Hampshire College; Brian Davis, Hill & Knowlton, Inc.; Nancy Dripps, American Sighthound Field Association; Donna Hawley, International Sled Dog Racing Association; Philip Hendry, International Sheepdog Society, Bedford, England; Bob Maida, Manassas, Virginia; Willie Necker, Wheeling, Illinois; Lori Scholz, The Seeing Eye.

Composition for DOGS ON DUTY by the Typographic section of National Geographic Production Services, Pre-Press Division. Printed and bound by Holladay-Tyler Printing Corp., Glenn Dale, Md. Film preparation by Catherine Cooke Studio, Inc., New York, N.Y. Color separations by the Lanman-Progressive Co., Washington, D. C.; Lincoln Graphics, Inc., Cherry Hill, N.J.; and NEC, Inc., Nashville, Tenn. Cover printed by Federated Lithographers-Printers, Inc., Providence, R.I. Teacher's Guide printed by McCollum Press, Inc., Rockville, Md.

Library of Congress CIP Data

O'Neill, Catherine
  Dogs on duty / by Catherine O'Neill
      p.   cm. — (Books for world explorers)
  Bibliography: p.
  Includes index.
  SUMMARY: Describes the ways in which dogs are bred and trained for such careers as livestock guardian, herder, helper for the disabled, sled-puller, and entertainer.
  ISBN 0-87044-659-2 :   ISBN 0-87044-664-9 (lib. bdg.) :
  1. Working dogs—juvenile literature. [1. Working dogs. 2. Dogs.] I. Title. II Series.
  SF428.2.054   1988
  636.7'0886—dc19   88-15933
                                         CIP
                                         AC

DOGS ON DUTY

BY CATHERINE O'NEILL

PUBLISHED BY
THE NATIONAL GEOGRAPHIC SOCIETY
WASHINGTON, D. C.

Gilbert M. Grosvenor, *President and Chairman of the Board*
Melvin M. Payne, Thomas W. McKnew, *Chairmen Emeritus*
Owen R. Anderson, *Executive Vice President*
Robert L. Breeden, *Senior Vice President
Publications and Educational Media*

PREPARED BY THE SPECIAL PUBLICATIONS
AND SCHOOL SERVICES DIVISION

Donald J. Crump, *Director*
Philip B. Silcott, *Associate Director*
Bonnie S. Lawrence, *Assistant Director*

BOOKS FOR WORLD EXPLORERS

Pat Robbins, *Editor*
Ralph Gray, *Editor Emeritus*
Ursula Perrin Vosseler, *Art Director*
Margaret McKelway, *Associate Editor*

STAFF FOR *DOGS ON DUTY*

Margaret McKelway, *Managing Editor*
Veronica J. Morrison, *Illustrations Editor*
Mary Elizabeth Molloy, *Art Director*
M. Linda Lee, *Researcher*
Kathryn N. Adams, Sandra F. Lotterman,
Editorial Assistants
Jennie H. Proctor, *Illustrations Assistant*
Janet A. Dustin, *Art Secretary*

ENGRAVING, PRINTING, AND PRODUCT MANUFACTURE: George V. White, *Manager*; Vincent P. Ryan, *Assistant Manager*; David V. Showers, *Production Manager*; Lewis R. Bassford, *Production Project Manager*; Kathie Cirucci, Timothy H. Ewing, *Senior Production Assistants*; Kevin Heubusch, *Production Assistant*; Carol R. Curtis, *Senior Production Staff Assistant.*

STAFF ASSISTANTS: Aimée Clause, Marisa Farabelli, Mary Elizabeth House, Kaylene F. Kahler, Karen Katz, Eliza C. Morton, Dru Stancampiano, Nancy J. White

INDEX: Maureen Walsh